TIBET A Hidde
The Newark

■ Pomegranate Artbooks ■ San Francisco ■

Pomegranate Artbooks
Box 6099
Rohnert Park, CA 94927

Pomegranate Europe Ltd.
Fullbridge House, Fullbridge
Maldon, Essex CM9 7LE
England

ISBN 0-87654-903-2
Pomegranate Catalog No. A840

Pomegranate publishes books of
postcards on a wide range of subjects.
Please write to the publisher for more information.

Designed by Young Jin Kim
Printed in Korea

06 05 04 03 02 01 00 99 98 97   11 10 9 8 7 6 5 4 3 2

To facilitate detachment of the postcards from this book, fold each card along its perforation line before tearing.

For centuries Tibet, the "Land of Snows," was hidden from the world by the towering peaks of the Himalayas. Situated in the heart of Asia at a mean altitude of 14,000 feet, this small, self-sufficient country was isolated by climate and terrain yet irrevocably linked with its immediate neighbors by ethnic, cultural, and religious ties. Until relatively recently, Tibet's spectacular geography, traditional lifestyle, and unique form of Buddhism were virtually unknown to the Western world.

Prior to 1959, Tibetans enjoyed a simple agricultural and nomadic lifestyle unchanged since the Middle Ages. To reach neighboring towns or to trade with China and India, Tibetans walked or rode yaks, mules, or horses; rivers were crossed in yak-skin boats or bridged with cantilevered plank or rope suspension structures. Beautifully adjusted to the rocky landscape, Tibetan architecture was in organic harmony with its environment. The massive strength of the architecture was relieved by colorful painted designs of Buddhist emblems, flowers, and folk tales on the wooden trim of windows, doors, and lintels. This light touch was further enhanced during festivals and holidays, when private homes and monasteries were decked with awnings, banners, and flowers.

The Tibetan people's active engagement with the spiritual world existed on several levels, from daily use of prayer flags, prayer wheels, rosaries, and charm boxes to participation in the great festivals of the yearly cycle celebrating the New Year, saints' days, and harvests. These ceremonies, performed by Buddhist monks, involved chanting, music, dancing, and presentation of special ritual objects. Giant paintings, appliqués, and images could be viewed, circumambulated, and perhaps touched at this time. Scriptures were recited and morality plays presented. The power and magnificence of the Buddhist faith, and the hierarchy that explained and preserved that faith, were thus made manifest, renewing and reinforcing the Tibetans' daily devotions.

This unique civilization has been irrevocably altered by political events of the twentieth century. Tibet has been incorporated into China, disrupting traditional Tibetan culture and forcing the exodus of countless Tibetans from their homeland. Tragically, Tibet's rich culture and Buddhist-centered society no longer exist. The Newark Museum's archives of photographs and Tibetan artifacts, amassed through purchases and gifts over the years and including objects of everyday life, paintings, sculptures, and ritual materials, thus comprises a valuable record of a civilization that is now vastly altered. The photographs in this book of postcards, from the collection of The Newark Museum, offer a rare glimpse of the rich cultural heritage of the Tibetan people.

TIBET: A Hidden World, 1905–1935

Boundary marker with prayer stones and flags; areas of
Kham designated as Chinese administrative districts by Chao
Er Feng in 1911. Photograph by Albert L. Shelton, c. 1913.

POMEGRANATE

BOX 6099

ROHNERT PARK CA 94927

TIBET: A Hidden World, 1905–1935

The Thirteenth Dalai Lama. Portrait taken in the studio of
Th. Paar, Darjeeling, during the Dalai Lama's stay there,
c. 1910–1912.

POMEGRANATE BOX 6099 ROHNERT PARK CA 94927

TIBET: A Hidden World, 1905–1935

Chortens (sacred structures), Kham. Photograph by Albert L. Shelton, c. 1905–1920.

POMEGRANATE BOX 6099 ROHNERT PARK CA 94927

TIBET: A Hidden World, 1905–1935

The Great Chorten of Gyantse, founded in 1427. Photograph
by C. Suydam Cutting, 1930.

POMEGRANATE   BOX 6099   ROHNERT PARK   CA   94927

TIBET: A Hidden World, 1905–1935

The Potala (Dalai Lama's residence), Lhasa, during the New
Year procession. Photograph by Ovshe Norzunov, c. 1900.

POMEGRANATE BOX 6099 ROHNERT PARK CA 94927

TIBET: A Hidden World, 1905–1935

The High Lama of Batang, Jö Lama at left, Batang, Kham.
Photograph by Albert L. Shelton, c. 1920.

POMEGRANATE BOX 6099 ROHNERT PARK CA 94927

TIBET: A Hidden World, 1905–1935

Tsogchen Dukhang (chapel), Sera monastery, founded 1419, Lhasa. Photograph early twentieth century (photographer unknown).

POMEGRANATE   BOX 6099   ROHNERT PARK   CA   94927

TIBET: A Hidden World, 1905–1935

Appliquéd banner displayed each New Year for Monlam
Chemo (Great Prayer Festival), Labrang, Amdo. Photograph
by M. G. Griebenow, c. 1922–1940.

POMEGRANATE   BOX 6099   ROHNERT PARK   CA   94927

TIBET: A Hidden World, 1905–1935

Harvest Festival, Milarepa play, dancing between dialogues,
Batang, Kham. Photograph by Roderick A. MacLeod,
c. 1920–1930.

POMEGRANATE BOX 6099 ROHNERT PARK CA 94927

TIBET: A Hidden World, 1905–1935

Yak caravan ("house yaks" indicated by nose rings) used for
local transport, Kham-Sichuan border. Photograph by Albert
L. Shelton, c. 1908–1920.

POMEGRANATE   BOX 6099   ROHNERT PARK, CA 94927

TIBET: A Hidden World, 1905–1935

King of Derge with his family while under house arrest in
Batang, Kham. Photograph by Albert L. Shelton, c. 1913.

POMEGRANATE   BOX 6099   ROHNERT PARK, CA 94927

TIBET: A Hidden World, 1905–1935

Shigatse Dzong (royal fortress), built by the Tsang king c.
1635 and the site of the Fifth Dalai Lama's enthronement in
1642. Photograph by C. Suydam Cutting, 1935.

POMEGRANATE BOX 6099 ROHNERT PARK CA 94927

TIBET: A Hidden World, 1905–1935

Thirteenth Dalai Lama's summer palace, Seshi Palber,
Chansal Linga, Norbu Linga, Lhasa. Photograph by
C. Suydam Cutting, 1935 or 1937.

POMEGRANATE BOX 6099 ROHNERT PARK CA 94927

TIBET: A Hidden World, 1905–1935

View of Gyantse; religious enclave on hill, market in
foreground. Photograph by C. Suydam Cutting, 1930.

POMEGRANATE BOX 6099 ROHNERT PARK CA 94927

TIBET: A Hidden World, 1905–1935

Ceremonial tent set up for review of honor guard by the Teji
(governor) of Markham. The Teji is seated, second from left;
his wife is seated, second from right. Photograph by Albert L.
Shelton, 1919.

POMEGRANATE BOX 6099 ROHNERT PARK CA 94927

TIBET: A Hidden World, 1905–1935

Amdo dignitaries assembled for a formal portrait. Apa Alo
seated, second from left. Photograph by M. G. Griebenow,
c. 1930.

POMEGRANATE   BOX 6099   ROHNERT PARK   CA   94927

TIBET: A Hidden World, 1905–1935

Two Yasor officials (seated) with attendants during New Year's Festival, Lhasa. Photographer and date unknown.

POMEGRANATE BOX 6099 ROHNERT PARK, CA 94927

TIBET: A Hidden World, 1905–1935

Monks blowing trumpets on a monastery roof, Lhasa.
Photograph by C. Suydam Cutting, 1937.

POMEGRANATE BOX 6099 ROHNERT PARK CA 94927

TIBET: A Hidden World, 1905–1935

Gartok monastery, showing a typically Tibetan assemblage of chapels, assembly halls, and apartments on a steep mountain slope, Mar Kham. Photograph by Albert L. Shelton, 1917.

POMEGRANATE BOX 6099 ROHNERT PARK CA 94927

TIBET: A Hidden World, 1905–1935

Monks working on a colored sand mandala, Drepung
monastery, Lhasa. Photograph by C. Suydam Cutting, 1937.

POMEGRANATE BOX 6099 ROHNERT PARK CA 94927

TIBET: A Hidden World, 1905–1935

The artist Tsering completing a tanka in commemoration of
the Thirteenth Dalai Lama, Norbu Linga, Lhasa. Photograph
by C. Suydam Cutting, 1937.

POMEGRANATE BOX 6099 ROHNERT PARK CA 94927

TIBET: **A Hidden World, 1905–1935**

Chinese and Tibetan porters carrying a litter over a rocky
pass, Sino-Tibetan border. Photograph by Albert L. Shelton,
1904.

POMEGRANATE BOX 6099 ROHNERT PARK CA 94927

TIBET: A Hidden World, 1905–1935

The Batang valley, with its meandering river and the town of
Batang, Kham. Photograph by Albert L. Shelton, 1907–1910.

POMEGRANATE BOX 6099 ROHNERT PARK CA 94927

TIBET: A Hidden World, 1905–1935

Kham village, with terraced fields and high-rise buildings.
Photograph by Albert L. Shelton, 1907–1910.

POMEGRANATE   BOX 6099   ROHNERT PARK   CA   94927

TIBET: A Hidden World, 1905–1935

Appliquéd white tents around the central players' platform for the annual Autumn Festival in Batang, Kham. Photograph by Albert L. Shelton, 1907–1920.

POMEGRANATE BOX 6099 ROHNERT PARK CA 94927

TIBET: A Hidden World, 1905–1935

The Jö Lama (center) and his parents in front of their yak-hair tent, Kham. Photograph by Albert L. Shelton, c. 1909.

POMEGRANATE   BOX 6099   ROHNERT PARK   CA   94927

TIBET: A Hidden World, 1905–1935
Men and women threshing grain on the roof of a house,
Kham. Photograph by Albert L. Shelton, 1907–1920.

POMEGRANATE BOX 6099 ROHNERT PARK CA 94927

TIBET: A Hidden World, 1905–1935

A yak caravan passing by the outer walls of Derge
monastery, Kham. Photograph by Albert L. Shelton,
1907–1920.

POMEGRANATE BOX 6099 ROHNERT PARK CA 94927

TIBET: A Hidden World, 1905–1935

Litang monastery, on the route between Batang and
Tatsienlu, Kham. Photograph by Albert L. Shelton,
1907–1920.

POMEGRANATE   BOX 6099   ROHNERT PARK   CA   94927

TIBET: A Hidden World, 1905–1935

Prayer wheels erected around a temple in Derge monastery,
Kham. Photograph by Albert L. Shelton, 1907–1920.

POMEGRANATE   BOX 6099   ROHNERT PARK   CA   94927